Green Jujitsu:

The Smart Way to Embed Sustainability into Your Organisation

Gareth Kane

Terra Infirma Ltd, gareth@terrainfirma.co.uk

First published in 2012 by Dō Sustainability

87 Lonsdale Road, Oxford OX2 7ET, UK

ISBN 978-1-909293-07-6 (eBook-ePub)

ISBN 978-1-909293-08-3 (eBook-PDF)

ISBN 978-1-909293-06-9 (Paperback)

A catalogue record for this title is available from the British Library.

At Dō Sustainability we strive to minimize our environmental impacts and carbon footprint through reducing waste, recycling and offsetting our CO_2 emissions, including those created through publication of this book. For more information on our environmental policy see **www.dosustainability.com**.

Page design and typesetting by Alison Rayner

Cover by Becky Chilcott

For further information on Dō Sustainability, visit our website: **www.dosustainability.com**

DōShorts

Dō Sustainability is the publisher of **DōShorts**: short, high-value ebooks that distil sustainability best practice for busy professionals. Each DōShort addresses one sustainability challenge at a time and can be read in 90 minutes.

Be the first to hear about new DōShorts

Our monthly newsletter includes links to all new and forthcoming DōShorts. We also link to a free extract from each new DōShort in our newsletter, and to blogs by our expert authors. Sign up for the newsletter at **www.dosustainability.com**.

Recently published and forthcoming titles you'll hear about include:

- *Promoting Sustainable Behaviour: A Practical Guide to What Works*
- *Sustainable Transport Fuels Business Briefing*
- *How to Make your Company a Recognised Sustainability Champion*
- *Product Sustainability*
- *Corporate Climate Change Adaptation*
- *Making the Most of Standards*
- *Sustainability Reporting for Small and Medium-sized Enterprises*
- *The Changing Profile of Corporate Climate Change Risk*
- *Solar Photovoltaics: Business Briefing*
- *Green Jujitsu: The Smart Way to Embed Sustainability into Your Organisation*
- *The First 100 Days on the Job: How to Plan, Prioritise and Build a Sustainable Organisation*

Write for us, or suggest a DōShort

Please visit **www.dosustainability.com** for our full publishing programme. If you don't find what you need, write for us! Or Suggest a DōShort on our website.

We look forward to hearing from you!

Abstract

BUSINESS HAS RECENTLY WOKEN UP to the need to address environmental sustainability in a meaningful way. No longer is it sufficient to have an environmental policy or environmental management system – substantial changes to business practice are required. Culture change is widely regarded as the most vital and the most difficult element of this paradigm shift. The standard methods of 'switch it off' stickers, awareness presentations and proclamations from the top have proved incapable of delivering the shift in attitudes required. Green Jujitsu is a completely different way of looking at culture change for environmental sustainability. Instead of trying to correct your colleagues' perceived 'weaknesses', it focuses instead on playing to their strengths to get them truly interested and engaged. This principle is applied to the 'elephant model' of culture change: providing clear guidance, inspiring people emotionally and altering the working environment. These techniques are illustrated with case studies from the author's own experience of facilitating culture change on the front line in some of the world's leading organisations.

About The Author

 **GARETH KANE** is an internationally recognised environmental and sustainability expert. He has appeared as a media pundit on sustainability issues on, for example, the BBC Six O'Clock News, Countryfile, The Politics Show and local radio. In 2008 The Journal newspaper named Gareth as a 'Rising Star, Future Leader' for his work on sustainability.

Gareth's consultancy Terra Infirma has a client list including the BBC, BAE Systems plc, Johnson Matthey plc, the NHS and East Coast Mainline. In June 2010 the company was singled out for praise in the press by UK Environment Secretary, the Rt Hon Caroline Spelman MP. Terra Infirma's Green Academy online training programme has attracted participants from around the globe – from the USA to New Zealand.

Gareth was elected onto Newcastle City Council in 2004. Until 2011, he was deputy Executive Member for Environment and Sustainability which culminated in Newcastle being declared the UK's most sustainable city by Forum for the Future in 2009 and 2010. He is now opposition spokesman on Sustainability.

Gareth is the author of two books on business and sustainability, most recently *The Green Executive*.

Contents

INTRODUCTION

What Is The Biggest Barrier To Corporate Sustainability?

THIS IS A QUESTION I AM OFTEN ASKED from the floor at speaking engagements. My answer is a little trite but very true: 'The biggest barrier is only six inches wide – it's the space between our ears.'

The root cause of much unsustainable practice is *attitude* – lack of priority, busy-ness, ignorance, habit, short-sightedness, despondence, fear, laziness or combinations of the above. Bad attitude seems to get worse exponentially with the size of the business – sustainable energy expert Amory Lovins has said that while 'primitive' animals like ants have communities which exhibit intelligence way beyond that of the sum of the individuals, the more humans you group together, the more stupid their combined behaviour[1].

When we think about environmental sustainability we tend to envision shiny new technology such as solar panels and electric vehicles. However, it has been estimated that 60–70% of internal environmental improvements are dependent on getting staff to change their behaviour[2]. When I visit clients it is all too common to see heating and air-conditioning switched on at the same time, hosepipes left running but stuck down a drain, valuable packaged products damaged by forklift trucks and potentially green technologies like teleconferencing facilities gathering dust. And beyond that, more substantial environmental improvements such as redesigning products and greening the supply chain depend on a proper culture of sustainability integrated throughout the organisation.

Changing the culture of an organisation is one of the key management challenges. When it is done correctly, the results can be dramatic. The uptake of Total Quality Management (TQM) in Japan has led to the country leading in the motor vehicle and photographic/optical equipment sectors, despite having no natural resources and very high labour costs. One of the key planks of TQM is that quality becomes everyone's responsibility – it needs to be embedded into the organisation.

Figure 1 shows my sustainability maturity model for organisations.

FIGURE 1. Sustainability maturity model.

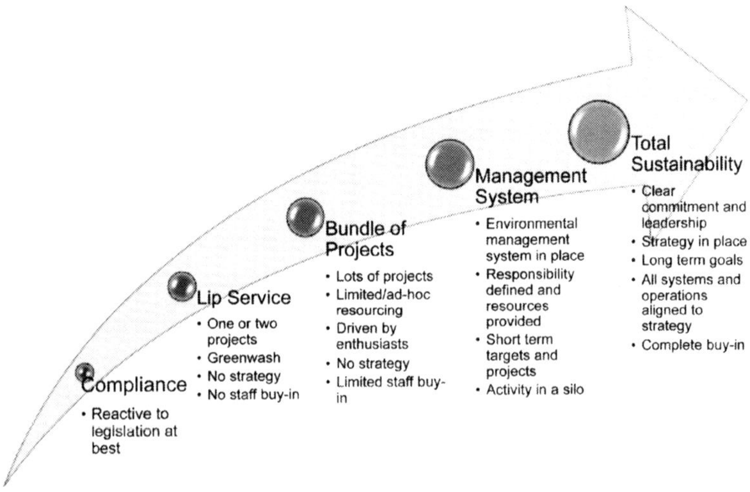

The stages are largely self-explanatory and the challenge for most organisations is to make the leap from the 'Management Systems' level, where environmental issues are 'managed' in a green silo, up to 'Total Sustainability' where sustainability is embedded into the organisation.

One of the biggest differences between the top two levels is making sustainability everyone's responsibility – just like quality under TQM. This manifests itself in the attitude of employees. I can tell very quickly which businesses 'get it' and which don't by a few conversations with staff members.

However, this is one area where many organisations struggle – culture change is very difficult and many simply try 'me-too' solutions such as awareness posters and environmental champions without properly thinking through what has to be done. This e-book proposes a smarter way of approaching culture change, bringing people along with you and playing to their strengths rather than trying to browbeat them into submission. There is a parallel here between boxing and jujitsu – in the former you try to overpower your opponent, in the latter you use people's strengths to get them where you want them. We will be considering this analogy in more detail in Chapter 2, but first we will look at problems faced by most conventional environmental sustainability programmes.

CHAPTER 1

Why Sustainability Programmes Fail

What's the problem?

I DIAGNOSE THE MOST COMMON BARRIERS in environmental sustainability programmes as:

- Lack of leadership: leadership is critical to any successful corporate programme and a lack of leadership will kill off culture change programmes before they get going.

- A lack of integration: 'green' and 'sustainability' are seen as tangential issues to the mainstream business processes and are thus of secondary importance or someone else's problem.

- A misalignment of responsibility and authority: most environmental managers have lots of responsibility and precious little authority. Conversely, people who have the power to push sustainability are given no responsibility to do so.

- A lack of accountability: environmental performance is left outside the performance management system.

- Wishful or limited thinking: 'We've appointed energy champions. Job done.'

- Sloppy company culture in general: I find that the companies who have a poor sustainability culture usually have poor discipline, weak quality standards and messy premises.

- A lack of empowerment: 'It's more than my job's worth to turn that off.'

- Ignorance: 'If I turn up the thermostat, the office will warm more quickly.'

- Inertia: 'We've always designed our products like that.' 'That sound? That's always there. No, we don't check our compressed air system for leaks. Should we?', etc.

- Fear: 'If we try this, who'll get the blame if it goes wrong?'

You will notice that these are predominantly about attitude and culture – very rarely is the real reason money. Northern Foods have saved many millions of pounds in energy and waste costs and they say 60–70% of it was achieved through low or no-cost behavioural changes[2].

I say again that the true barrier to sustainability is about six inches wide – the space between our ears. Most of the problems and solutions can be found there.

Why 'switch it off' doesn't work

The traditional approach to behavioural change has been to slather 'switch it off' stickers and posters over every switch, wall and machine. If culture change was that easy, you wouldn't be reading this e-book.

I once worked with a company which had A3 posters on sustainability in every hallway and foyer. Each sheet was packed with text on company policy. As an experiment I asked one workshop contingent whether they knew the company's definition of sustainability. No-one did. I asked if anyone had read the statement. No-one had. There was nothing in this communication to encourage anyone to read. It was a complete waste of time and effort.

So why doesn't it work?

- The injunctions to act get lost amongst the noise of the multitude of messages we are bombarded with every day.

- People generally resent being hectored and may resist as a reflex reaction.

- There's no explanation of the benefits of this action either to the individual, the business or wider society.

- Familiarity breeds contempt – you soon stop noticing the signs and posters.

- The message is usually uninspiring, lifeless and dull.

At best, these programmes are launched because of a lack of imagination. At worst, they are for the ego of the originator rather than the intended audience. A prime suspect is the ubiquitous 'Please consider the impact on the environment before printing this email' line in email signature blocks, which is clearly there to say 'I think I'm morally superior to you.'

Institutional inertia

I have already quoted Amory Lovins saying that animals like ants have communities which exhibit intelligence way beyond that of the sum of the individuals, but the more humans you group together, the more stupid the combined behaviour (or words to that effect). As an optimist, I like to think of this phenomenon as 'institutional inertia' rather than group stupidity. My definition of institutional inertia is:

> *The more people you get together,*
> *the harder it is to effect change.*

You can see this if you go on holiday with a group of friends and try to decide which restaurant to eat at one evening. The length of time it takes to make the decision and act increases exponentially with the number of people involved. If you are a couple, you'll probably be onto your coffee before a group of eight has sat down.

When you scale this up to the organisational level a huge number of factors kick in: internal politics, factionalism, fear of failure, fear to speak up, fear of standing out, the desire to belong, tradition (aka 'the way it's done round here'), formal and informal hierarchies, etc., etc. – they all add up to considerable inertia.

The challenge of overcoming this inertia – 'turning the supertanker around' – is immense. In my experience, the most important factors are strong, consistent leadership and a somewhat counter-intuitive combination of bone-headed determination and nimble culture change techniques. This e-book will help you with the latter, but the others have to come from within.

How not to do culture change

There are a number of pitfalls that many people fall into when trying to change the culture in organisations:

- Preaching: preaching doesn't work. It is as simple as that. The temptation to preach is very strong, in particular amongst those of us who feel very strongly about environmental issues. But it is counter-productive and simply switches people off.

- Irrelevance: talking about the plight of the polar bear or orang-utan may get people's sympathy, but both are too far removed from the everyday experience of your staff to make them want to change the way they behave. In general, in my sessions I only mention the scale of environmental impacts in passing to put solutions in context.

- Eco-clichés: despite my long campaign against them, there is still a prevalence of eco-clichés in imagery in green messages. Pictures of hands cupping saplings make me want to scream and they send out the subconscious message 'here's the worthy but dull bit, normal service will continue shortly'.

- Not getting leadership fully signed up: leadership is a key plank of culture change. Unfortunately, many CEOs are scared of the sustainability agenda and have a tendency to disappear whenever the topic is debated.

- Unintended consequences of incentives: take care with financial incentives as they can produce all sorts of unintended consequences and it is possible to stir up resentment accidentally. Some issues, for example, staff parking, raise passions way beyond what they logically should.

- Not realigning other systems such as human resources policies so they promote a more sustainable culture. We will look at this in more detail in Chapters 5 and 6.

- Taking your foot off the pedal: the secret of success in fostering green behaviour is to keep going.

- Cognitive dissonance: this occurs when we try and hold two conflicting ideas in our heads at the same time. For example, if you try to foster a culture where sustainability is strong, then ask employees to take clearly unsustainable actions, they will get confused and cynical.

Questions for you

How would you rate your culture of sustainability from 1–5, where 1 means no culture at all and 5 means everyone understands what sustainability means to them?

Why do you rate the company like this?

What tone does your sustainability programme currently take?

How relevant is it to the day-to-day activities of your employees?

CHAPTER 2

The Green Jujitsu Approach

The jujitsu analogy

SO, GIVEN THAT WE HAVE SEEN that culture change for sustainability is very difficult, how do we make sustainability stick? The answer is to harness the strengths of your employees rather than focusing on their weaknesses.

The analogy that spans this e-book is the difference between boxing and the martial art of jujitsu. Boxing involves standing toe to toe with your opponent and trying to batter the living daylights out of them – before they do the same to you. Such a war of attrition will be familiar to many, if not all, sustainability practitioners.

Jujitsu, however, is about using your opponent's strength, energy and momentum against them and levering them into submission. I'm not going to stretch the analogy too thin – there is no deeper philosophical or technical similarity between embedding sustainability and a martial art – in fact, seeing your employees as 'opponents' won't do your efforts much good. But the idea of bringing people with you by understanding their strengths and weaknesses is an extremely powerful one as we shall see.

In the rest of this e-book, we will be considering this approach to embedding environmental sustainability into the culture of the organisation. Simple changes, such as changing a statement into a question, can increase your likelihood of success by a remarkable degree.

Understanding attitudes to sustainability

Attitudes towards the environment and concepts such as sustainable development vary across a wide spectrum. As in any relationship, it is important to understand the other party's point of view or 'where they are coming from' to build mutual respect. Conversely, completely

....

FIGURE 2. Attitudes to the environment and sustainability.

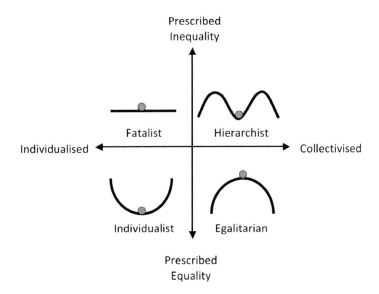

SOURCE: Adapted from Thompson, M., Ellis, R. and Widavsky, A. 1990. *Cultural Theory* (Boulder, CO: Westview Press).

....

different attitudes to the same problem or issue often cause conflict and rancour. So it is worth considering different attitudes to environmental sustainability.

Many social scientists use the model in Figure 2 to categorise attitudes to society and nature[3], each attitude being defined by the degree of equality/inequality and individualism/collectivism. The model uses a red ball representing the state of the environment on a surface. If the red ball is moved a small amount (an environmental impact), then it will either stay where it is (another stable state), return to its original position (resilient to change), or drop off the model (ecological breakdown).

The four attitudes are:

1. Individualists believe that the planet is robust and there to be exploited. This is the typical belief of free marketeers and so-called 'climate change deniers'.

2. Hierarchists believe the environment is there to be exploited within limits. This is the typical approach of governments and public sector bodies.

3. Egalitarians believe that the environment is fragile and requires protection. Environmental damage must be minimised at all costs. Typical approach of environmental pressure groups.

4. Fatalists don't have a view on whether any state of the environment is better or worse on any other state – the whole debate passes them by.

These are caricatures of course, but they help explain why, say, if you present a randomly selected group of people with analytical data on an environmental problem such as climate change, some will accept it (hierarchists), some will say it is exaggerated (individualists), some will say you aren't taking the risk seriously enough (egalitarians) and others will simply shrug (fatalists).

Internal resistance

The jujitsu approach requires us to understand and overcome resistance to sustainability. Resistance to sustainability from individuals can come in a number of forms:

- Anti-green sentiments: as we saw above, many people (individualists) find the idea of natural limits is anathema to their world view and, at worst, some pernicious form of communism in disguise.

- Narrow economic focus: 'sustainability is not a business issue and should be left to politicians'. This tends to go hand in hand with the individualist approach above.

- 'Too busy/not my problem': this is often a problem in middle management where individuals have many competing requirements for their attention.

- Limited ambition: 'OK, we've got ISO14001 certification, what more do you want?'

- Fear for the future: sustainability requires new ways of working which in turn requires risk taking. Many people are highly risk averse and resist change for the sake of it, but others may fear that their skills will become redundant in the new regime.

- Staff/management friction: staff members and/or their unions may believe that sustainability programmes will benefit the managerial classes but not people at the front line.

To use the jujitsu approach we have to recognise and understand these, while never accepting them as permanent obstacles. They can be overcome.

Motivations of different roles

Different job roles bring with them different priorities which must also be taken into consideration, for example:

- Boardroom/senior management: concerned with strategic opportunities and risks, brand protection and competitive advantage.

- Middle management: concerned with meeting short-/medium-term targets, delivering individual projects and managing costs. People at this level are often very aware of their own career prospects.

- Frontline staff: often detached from the corporate core in larger organisations. Their loyalty often lies with their immediate team rather than the organisation as a whole.

In addition, different types of staff will respond to different forms of information and approaches, for example:

- Technical staff: comfortable with data, graphs and charts – and will always want to see such evidence before acting. Give them a problem and they will want to find a solution.

- Financial staff: will respond best to financial data and cost/benefit analyses.

- Administrative staff: often ask 'how is this relevant to me?' A key strategy is to use human interest stories (see Chapter 3).

So if you want to engage frontline non-technical staff and senior financial directors, you will need to take quite different approaches.

The elephant model of culture change

My favoured model for the art of culture change uses the analogy of an elephant guided by a human rider walking along a path and was popularised by Dan and Chip Heath[4]. The direction the elephant takes is determined by three things: instructions provided to the elephant by the rider, the desires of the elephant itself and the nature of the path. The elements translate as:

- The rider is the logical, conscious part of our minds.

- The elephant is our subconscious – which is usually the strongest influence on our behaviour whether we like it or not.

- The path is the environment we operate in, with easier and more difficult routes, and distractions along the way.

To change the direction the elephant is travelling, we must provide clear instructions to the rider, engage emotionally with the elephant, and shape the path to 'nudge' people into following desired behaviour patterns. The following sections demonstrate how to apply the Green Jujitsu concept to each of these three culture change elements.

No pain, no gain

We mentioned in the last chapter that a common pitfall was to take your foot off the gas and assume the job has been done in one pass. When learning any martial art, part of the process is to repeat physical movements until they become instinctive. In the same way, you must train yourself and your organisation again and again until sustainability becomes instinctive. But even if you get to black belt in a martial art, if you stop training you will slowly lose the reflexes and fitness that got you there. Likewise with culture change, the new culture must be constantly reinforced to keep it as the predominant way of doing things.

Questions for you

Who are you trying to engage with?

What role(s) do they perform in the organisation?

What might put them off the sustainability agenda?

What turns them on?

CHAPTER 3

Providing Information

THE FIRST ELEMENT OF THE ELEPHANT MODEL of culture change is how to effectively communicate information to the rider and thus to the elephant. We have seen in Chapter 1 that most organisations find it very difficult to do this properly – the ubiquitous 'switch it off' sticker has failed to make an impact and they often struggle to know what to do next. Under the Green Jujitsu approach we need to think very carefully about the audience and tailor the message to appeal to them.

Fighting for attention

The main problem with giving instructions is information overload. Check out the notice board of any organisation and you will see 'death by poster' – 101 different instructions on everything from health and safety to the latest charity fundraising all desperately clamouring for the attention of passers-by. Add a poster on sustainability and it just becomes another voice lost in the babble.

A number of tactics are often used to get the message heard:

- Shock tactics: UK military bases used to use images of scantily clad women tripping on hazards to attract the attention of servicemen to health and safety messages. Such imagery is unacceptable by modern standards and in any case soon loses its impact.

- Guerrilla marketing: get your message posted in places where it is unexpected and you get a captive audience – for example, on the back of a toilet cubicle door.

- Interrupt your audience: a number of online marketing ventures involve an advert being played before a video or before an online article – again this can lead to annoying people rather than inspiring them.

Whichever approach you take, all you are doing is trying to shout louder than everyone else in a room full of people shouting. The Green Jujitsu approach doesn't require volume, but tailors the message so the audience wants to listen to it.

What is relevant to your audience?

So we need a message which is clear, concise and relevant to the audience. A vital pre-requisite is to find out what makes the audience tick and then package the message appropriately.

For example, my friend and colleague Graeme Mills of GPM Network was given the task of persuading employees of a regeneration charity to switch their computers off at night. When Graeme ran some focus groups, he found that those employees were so focused on their worthy projects, they tended to see other issues as a distraction. Graeme decided to tap into this narrow focus and developed a campaign where the PC screensavers told them 'if you switch off this computer every night, it saves the equivalent of making a £57 annual donation to our projects'. To employees, this was a significant personal donation, so switching off became a painless way to contribute to frontline projects.

Speaking their language

Another key Green Jujitsu tactic is to match your language to the audience. Words such as 'carbon', 'environment' or 'green' can lead to people either reacting badly if they are anti-green or simply switching off if they don't see the relevance. Words like 'energy', 'waste' and 'risk' can be more powerful to the ears of the unconverted – and after all, those are the people you need to speak to. Table 1 has some suggestions of 'green language' that you might want to avoid for certain audiences and some 'jujitsu' alternatives that sometimes work better.

TABLE 1: Green and Jujitsu Language

Green language	Jujitsu language
Green	Waste
The environment	Energy efficiency
The planet	Resource efficiency
Sustainable development	Lean manufacturing
Sustainability	Productivity
Climate change	Return on investment
Global warming	Legislation
Carbon emissions	Pollution
Carbon footprint	Liabilities
Corporate social responsibility	Risk
Community	Energy security
	Costs and savings
	Product differentiation
	Market opportunity
	Hazardous
	Health & safety

Use questions, not statements

Bold statements of fact to a cynic or sceptic can be like a red rag to a bull. Others will simply ignore statements if they think the problem is irrelevant or too difficult. In contrast, asking questions (maybe with a fact embedded in the middle) tends to give you momentum, as questions are less threatening and your opponent has to respond thoughtfully[5].

I use this frequently in my workshops. I normally start each session with the question 'Why should your company be concerned about sustainability?' This throws the responsibility for arguing the business case onto the audience, forcing them to work it out for themselves. This is much more effective than me, a stranger, trying to persuade them they should be concerned.

The same approach can be taken day to day in meetings, for example:

- 'Our biggest customer has issued a press release saying they want to address the carbon footprint of their supply chain – how do we respond?'

- 'How robust is the business to rising oil prices?'

- 'Do you know that we are wasting £2,000,000 on energy every year?'

- 'How are we going to respond to the EU's latest product stewardship legislation?'

This approach is particularly effective with senior management, who often prefer to be consulted on their views rather than being presented with a *fait accompli*.

Reframing the argument

A common mistake is to rush into a debate where the 'frame' of the argument is working against you. Like a window frame restricting the view outside a room, the 'frame' of an argument restricts the scope of the debate. We often plunge into an argument using the default frame which may stack the odds against us. Instead it is important to step back, consider the big picture and choose the 'correct' frame.

For example, if you find yourself debating 'environment *or* profit' with a senior manager, you are unlikely to make much headway. Rather than trying to fight that battle, you need to reframe the discussion as 'environment *and* profit', and then you will find barriers starting to fall as your aims and the interests of the manager are aligned.

Reframing arguments often involves starting discussions correctly. If you ask 'Should we be tackling sustainability issues?', you are giving the other person permission to answer 'No!' If, however, you ask 'How should we go about tackling sustainability?', the frame has shifted to obscure that answer, making it much more difficult to be so negative.

Effective switch it off

While I have been dismissive of 'switch it off' labels, there is a role for such instructions if you flip the approach around. Instead of saying 'you must switch this off', you say 'you may switch this off, but not that'.

A good example of this has been developed by Northern Foods – an £1 billion a year producer of ready meals. The system uses a three-colour labelling scheme on all factory equipment. A red label means 'leave it on, whatever'; green means 'if this machine doesn't appear to be doing anything useful, switch it off'; and amber means 'if you think this machine should be switched off, check with your supervisor'. This clear and empowering system is easy for a low skilled workforce, many of whom do not have English as a first (or sometimes second) language.

Feedback

When I graduated from college, I lived in a dingy bedsit in London for the first winter until I could afford something better. The room had an old-style spinning disk electricity meter by the door, so every time I switched on the electric cooker or the electric fire, the disk would start spinning like mad. I remember this visual feedback of how fast my money was disappearing making me use those appliances very carefully (I found that making pasta or rice warmed the room better than the heater, so I used to cook as soon as I got in from work). It has been found that people with meters that provide them with feedback on electricity consumption use 4% less than they would without[6].

Feedback has long been used by industry to influence behaviour in many aspects of performance. Many factories display the time since the last accident by the gate and many display ranks of bar charts covering everything from quality pass/fail rates to staff absences.

Some companies who have advanced energy management system use real-time feedback. One example is a simple traffic light system to show if consumption is low (green), high (amber) or very high (red). This is a nice way of converting data into a form that staff can easily grasp and of course you can tighten the amber and red settings to encourage continual improvement.

Storytelling

If you look at any newsagent's shelf, many of the magazines will be dominated by true-life stories and personalities. If you switch on the TV news, no matter what the news item is, they will inevitably turn to someone affected for their views, no matter how tangential or inconsequential. Why? Because we like to hear stories from 'people like us'. Converting the message into a personal story is a powerful way of making it more engaging.

At defence giant BAE Systems plc, an enterprising engineer developed a way to apply the stop-start technology he witnessed in his son's car to the factory production lines. Stop-start technology allows a car engine to switch off during brief stops at, say, traffic lights, and then spring back to life in an instant. Adapting this concept to the production line has resulted in fantastic energy savings. As BAE Systems prides itself on technological innovation, this made a brilliant human-interest story in the company magazine. This is much more effective than empty statements of intent or statistics – people can see someone like them doing something and making a difference.

Similarly, lawyers Muckle LLP ran a story about an employee using shredded paper waste as bedding for her horses. 'Happy Horses and Reused Resources' was the headline. The picture of the employee and her happy horse was much more attractive to employees and external stakeholders than a picture of hands holding a planet.

Integration of messages

In one of my workshops, a manufacturing operative, straight off the factory floor and still wearing his dirty overalls, nailed a vital point:

We've got these stickers on the machines telling us to switch them off. But there's nothing in the standard operating procedures about it. It is hammered into us from day one to follow the SOPs, so, if we're not sure, we ignore the stickers. If you want it to happen, it should be in the SOPs.

If you have clear and established messaging channels, the sustainability message must be integrated into those channels. If it is outside those channels then it will remain on the periphery. So sustainability must be integrated into:

- Standard operating procedures.

- Induction training.

- Leaders' statements.

- Company reports.

- Company publications.

- Intranet/websites.

Questions for you

What message are you trying to communicate?

What are the most effective channels?

How can you integrate the message into key existing channels?

cont.

What language should you avoid? What language should you use instead?

How can you better frame the message?

What killer questions will help you open minds to sustainability?

How can you turn the sustainability message into human interest stories?

CHAPTER 4

Engaging Emotionally

LOOKING AT OUR ELEPHANT/RIDER/PATH culture change model, it is the elephant itself that makes the decisions at the end of the day. We like to think we are logical, rational beings, but every one of us is heavily swayed by gut instinct, personal values, irrational prejudices and past experiences both positive and negative. If, say, you want to buy a new car, you would probably analyse performance stats, features and prices and compare them with your needs and budget, but it is often the model you would like to be seen behind the wheel of that you end up choosing. It is this that makes us like Captain Kirk, not Mr Spock.

So how do you engage with the elephant and bring it around to your way of thinking? This is the core of the Green Jujitsu approach – how to tap emotionally into the employee's mind to change their behaviour.

Lead by example

It is very difficult to effect a positive culture change if the organisation's leadership is not on board. Good leadership inspires us and our inner elephants, makes us feel good about the work we do; bad leadership makes us cynical and resentful.

The greatest green business leader is undoubtedly the late Ray Anderson of modular flooring giant InterfaceFLOR. In 1996 he read a book called

The Ecology of Commerce that hit him 'like a spear in the chest'. He swiftly launched a programme called Mission Zero, the objective of which was to have a zero ecological footprint by 2020[7]. To his dying day in 2011, he relentlessly pursued this goal and made quite extraordinary achievements which have proved that business and sustainability were not incompatible.

Another great example is Sir Stuart Rose when he was Chairman and Chief Executive of British retail legend Marks & Spencer. The story goes that Rose saw a screening of Al Gore's documentary film *An Inconvenient Truth* and decided he must act on moral grounds. Insiders say that, as well as this desire to 'do the right thing', Rose was always highly conscious of Marks & Spencer's position as the most trusted brand on the high street and realised that sustainability was a key plank of trust in the 21st century. He made his commitment clear by setting up the Plan A sustainability programme ('because there is no Plan B') and funding it to the tune of £200 million[2].

There are two parts of such inspiring leadership – words and actions – and the two must match. In terms of words, a clear commitment must be made above and beyond the platitudes that most organisations pump out. Ray Anderson rarely spoke in public about anything other than corporate responsibility issues.

These words must be followed by actions, such as Rose's financial commitment. Consistency is a key factor in determining trust, so all business decisions must be as consistent as possible with the green commitment. Where this can't be done, decisions must be explained fully and, where feasible, 'offset' by a new environmental project.

Personal actions can help reinforce the idea that this commitment is not just skin-deep. Leaders can adopt green behaviour in their personal life by, for example, cycling to work, installing solar panels at home, or leading a group of volunteers to dig a pond. Mistakes that can damage personal reputation range from leaving lights on to turning up in a gas-guzzling company car.

The fallback plan: Guerrilla tactics

If you can't get such high-level buy-in for sustainability, all is not lost – you can launch an underground programme and build momentum until it is irresistible. There are myriad examples in history of where small, determined and resourceful bands of fighters have kept much more powerful armies at bay. Again, the Green Jujitsu principle applies – guerrillas who confront their opponents on a conventional battlefield will be annihilated.

The standard guerrilla approach is to get a team of enthusiasts together, then use Green Jujitsu techniques to build up enough projects to demonstrate to the leadership that sustainability is in the interest of the organisation. The use of Green Jujitsu language and questions that we saw in Chapter 3 will be vital weapons on this mission.

Tapping into company culture

Many organisations have a very strong formalised company culture. For example, Canon has a philosophy called 'kyosei' which translates as 'living and working together for the common good'. The company has subsumed sustainability into kyosei culture, a nice piece of Green Jujitsu.

Cultural norms can be less explicit than such a formal philosophy. The example of the standard operating procedures (SOPs) in the last chapter demonstrates this well. The culture in this company, where many of the materials are highly hazardous, was 'follow the SOPs' – if something isn't in the SOPs it is not part of company culture for manufacturing operatives. By embedding sustainability instructions into the SOPs, the company is working with the culture, not against it as it was with the contradictory switch it off labels.

Creating a brand new sustainability centre of gravity such as Marks and Spencer's Plan A is more difficult and risky. It is noticeable that Marks & Spencer is careful to blend Plan A into the mainstream. For example, Plan A communications use the same 'famous faces' as it uses in all its other advertising, creating a seamless continuum between the two. This sends a message to stakeholders inside and outside the company that sustainability is mainstream.

Building trust

Probably the most important factor in working with the elephant is trust. Our inner elephants are often cynical and suspicious, so trust is hard to win and easy to lose. Many of us will have been asked to take part in an exercise where the residual feeling was that we had been used simply to tick a box somewhere to say employees have been consulted and the key decisions had already been made. This kind of breach of trust – 'we want you to have your say, then we'll ignore it' – can completely undermine very hard won progress.

Leadership guru Warren Bennis[8] lists the most important factors influencing our trust as:

1. Competence: the technical and managerial competence to engage properly and deliver on promises.

2. Constancy: the degree to which the organisation/individual can be relied upon to do what it says it will do, even when the going gets tough.

3. Caring: that their welfare is of genuine concern to the organisation/individual.

4. Candour: openness, transparency and honesty, which we will discuss further below.

5. Congruity (or authenticity): that the individual is genuinely committed to what they say they want to do.

These five elements must be embedded into every aspect of the culture change programme. If your employees trust you then your job will be substantially easier.

Show, don't tell

In May 1997, I stood by a roadside in Arctic Russia and looked around at 360° of ecological destruction as far as my eyes could see. On the horizon, chimneys from a nickel smelter pumped sulphurous steam into the sky above me, which would fall as acid rain and scorch the land even more. That day I made a decision – I would dedicate my life to tackling man's impact on the planet. In 2010, *Daily Mail* Science Editor Michael Hanlon went on a trip to Greenland. Before this visit he had been sceptical about climate change, but when he saw the scale of the melt, he changed his mind[9].

Both of these Damascene moments were, strictly speaking, irrational. Before my Arctic experience, I had been an armchair environmentalist and accepted all the science of climate change and acidification. Hanlon had looked at the same information and distrusted it. What each of us witnessed was a tiny part of the world on a single day. I could have been looking at the only acid rain damage in the world and Hanlon could have simply seen normal seasonal ice melt. But that didn't matter. What we felt did. If you witness something with your own eyes, it is the most powerful persuader in the world.

While dragging your entire workforce off to see a glacier melt is beyond the scope of most organisations, you can use similar experiences to get your message across. If you want people to understand how much waste you produce, try piling it up in the car park or factory yard so they can see it for themselves. If you want to demonstrate energy losses then feeling the heat on your face is more powerful than a bar chart on a Powerpoint presentation.

Another option is to get employees involved in hands-on conservation projects. Digging ponds, planting trees and litter picking may be small scale on the grand scale of global environmental pressures, but they do give an experiential, kinaesthetic link between small-scale actions and the planet.

The next best thing to experiencing something yourself is hearing 'someone like you' talking about their experience of that thing. This is why the storytelling approach we looked at in the last chapter is so powerful.

'More stilettos than sandals'

The green movement has a well-earned reputation for presenting sustainability as the hair-shirt option. We are bombarded with litanies of how we should be ashamed of ourselves as a species, often by people who seem to be enjoying lecturing us. There may be some truth in what they say, but how they say it is a turn-off. Hands up who wants a guilt trip?

The answer is to make it fun: ditch the hair-shirt and make sustainability sexy. The 'more stilettos than sandals' maxim came from Ashley Lodge of Harper Collins[10] and it neatly sums up the idea of making sustainability attractive, positive and compelling, not a knotty issue of conscience. I mentioned before those annoying 'Please think about the environment and do not print this email' messages people add to their email signature block. Well, some creative and witty types have rewritten these to put a smile on the reader's face, for example 'Printing this email will make Al Gore cry'[11].

A particularly successful approach to making sustainability fun is to run competitions. Everyone loves a competition and it is very difficult to resist taking part. Lawyers Muckle LLP kicked off their environmental awareness campaign with a multiple choice quiz where employees have to guess the answers to questions such as 'how much paper does the company use per partner per month?' Employees were so shocked by the answer they went on to cut this by two-thirds. Muckle took this further to set an annual competition between the three floors of their offices to see who could best reduce carbon emissions. This approach has also been adopted by drinks giant Diageo, who run a competition between their sites around the globe. Taking part is mandatory and Gold, Silver and Bronze awards are given out to the best performers.

Make people part of the solution

Many staff engagement and culture change programmes see employees as part of the problem. They are not behaving as they should, therefore their behaviour must corrected – like naughty schoolchildren. This adversarial mindset does nothing to inspire the elephant and is the complete antithesis of the Green Jujitsu approach.

My favourite culture change technique is to flip this around and make employees part of the solution by getting them to generate ideas to help the programme. The strengths of this approach are:

- People feel they are being taken seriously.

- Individuals find it difficult to switch off in exercises – so you get more attention.

- You get automatic buy-in as people get excited about their ideas.

- You usually get some excellent new suggestions and will identify barriers to green behaviour.

- If and when those suggestions are implemented then they are more likely to be accepted by employees.

Anyone who has been on one of my training courses will almost certainly have been asked to apply the theory to their organisation. This approach empowers the employees, gives them a deeper understanding of the issues, creates buy-in and gives you a great source of ideas to boot. Annex A describes how I go about this in practice.

Incentives

I was in the middle of a series of assignments for a client with sites across the UK. I knew they were about to hit their annual energy saving target, but I didn't know they had given every employee gift vouchers as a reward. The difference between the sessions before and after the reward was palpable. Everyone was suddenly very interested in energy-saving. 'I feel really guilty – I didn't do anything to contribute to this', one woman told me. 'I suppose I'd better start!'

Incentives are very powerful if done properly, but they can be destructive if done badly. The last thing you want is individuals gaming the system to maximise reward while passing the problem onto others. A great example I have come across is a management consultancy who ran a paper saving competition between their teams. Whoever saved the most paper was able to donate their savings to the charity of their choice. This is very clever – it engaged the teams to act towards a virtuous end.

Teams and teamwork

What can a single designer do to change the lifecycle environmental performance of a complex product, say, a car? If they're really clever (or very lucky) that individual might come up with some revolutionary new aerodynamic tweak which leads to a huge improvement in fuel efficiency, but it is very unlikely. On the other hand, if the whole product development team is tasked with greening the vehicle, that's a different matter – they can determine the overall design concept, optimise every component and subsystems and exploit synergies between innovations.

Elephants are herd animals and prefer to move in groups. In the same way, we can use teams as an intermediary between the individual and the corporation as a whole. This has many opportunities:

- Empowerment: working together, the team has the power to actually change things.

- Purpose: at the team level, the relevance of sustainability to the job role is very tangible.

- Camaraderie: the team has a common mission and will help each other achieve it.

- Peer pressure: loyalty to fellow team members is often stronger than loyalty to the organisation overall.

While these are advantages, they can initially be barriers – sometimes it is hard to win over the trust of a tightly knit team and individual members can sometimes hide behind formal or informal leaders to avoid having to change. The best approach to overcome this is of course Green Jujitsu – working to strengths rather than weaknesses, for example:

- Tailor all sustainability communications to the team's role.

- Illustrate awareness material with case studies of team effort.

- Challenge the team to come up with sustainability solutions for their role.

- Give the team leader personal responsibility to deliver sustainability goals.

- Aim incentives and rewards at the team as a whole.

Questions for you

Are your leaders committed to sustainability?

If not, how can you use the techniques in Chapters 3 and 4 to get their commitment?

What positive aspects of company culture can you tap into?

How can you use 'show, don't tell' experiences to engage staff members?

Are your sustainability communications and programmes engaging and fun?

How can you utilise competitions and incentives to engage staff members?

Can you make your employees part of the solution?

How can you utilise teams within the organisation to maximise the effectiveness of your engagement?

CHAPTER 5

Nudging People Onto
The Right Path

PEOPLE (AND ELEPHANTS) TEND to take the path of least resistance to any goal. You only have to look at how people cut corners when walking along actual paths to create short cuts. While this is often seen as a problem, it can be harnessed to your advantage, shaping the path to encourage elephants to go where you'd like them to. The book *Nudge* popularised the idea of altering behaviour by making 'bad' behaviour difficult and 'good' behaviour easy by altering the 'architecture' of choices[12].

So to encourage sustainable behaviour you must make good behaviour easy (e.g. promote cycling to work by providing good quality, covered cycle racks plus showers and lockers) and 'bad' behaviour should be more difficult (e.g. charging for staff parking permits). This section looks at various options for embedding this kind of thinking into your organisation.

Providing green technology

An obvious pre-requisite of green behaviour is having the infrastructure available to allow that behaviour. This is analogous to the elephant having an alternative path in the first place – many organisations seem to expect individuals to make their own. Examples include:

- Teleconferencing facilities to eliminate unnecessary business travel.

- Telecommuting facilities along with policies to promote working from home.

- Low carbon vehicles.

- Water efficient facilities such as multi-flush toilets.

- Zoned heating and lighting to match work patterns so only the minimum needs to be switched on in any circumstances.

- Recycling facilities.

Of course, once you have provided the technology you have to use the other Green Jujitsu techniques to ensure that they are actually used.

You can take this a step further forward and use automation to take individuals out of the loop altogether. Automatic lighting, heating/ ventilation controls and IT systems (e.g. 'Nightwatchman' software) can all save energy in this way.

Changing the physical environment

When I first got started in this career, I routinely used to suggest to clients that if they really wanted to boost paper recycling in their offices they should take away everyone's general waste bins and give them a paper recycling bin. A general waste bin could be put in the corner of the office or at the end of the corridor – reversing standard practice where if people wanted to recycle, they had to trek to the recycling bin. In most cases those clients looked at me as if I were mad. Now this shift in bins is fast becoming standard practice.

This is a classic example of a nudge – rearranging the physical work environment to make green behaviour easier and 'bad' behaviour harder. Other examples include:

- Put cycle parking next to the front entrance, not at the far end of the car park.

- Likewise, place electric vehicle charging bays closer to the front door than other pool vehicles.

- Make it difficult to light an entire building with one switch, but easy to switch off lights all at once.

- Place staircases as a shorter and more obvious route than lifts in low rise buildings.

Policy changes

A 'perverse incentive' is policy which encourages people to do the 'wrong' thing. These must be hunted down and eliminated with extreme prejudice. In a recent engagement session I conducted at a major international company, someone complained that no-one was using the company's teleconferencing system. When we explored why not, we discovered that in order to calculate the financial benefits of the system the company made it a condition of booking that an estimation of avoided staff travel time and travel costs had to be provided. So you'd have to sit down and work out where everyone was coming from, how they were travelling, how long it would take them, what each person's hourly cost was and what fares/hire car charges/mileage they would incur. And then add it all up and then you could use the system. Most people are unfamiliar with teleconferencing, so by putting this extra burden on 'good' behaviour, staff were just sticking to the same old 'bad' behaviour they were used to – booking a conference room and letting everyone make their own travel arrangements. You can hardly blame them.

Where perverse incentives are found, they need to be flipped around to nudge people towards sustainable behaviour. Another client of mine changed their travel booking policy so that booking a train fare was done in house for you, but if you wanted a short-haul flight, you had to book and pay for it yourself and claim back the cost. So while you still had the choice, it was much more of a hassle to fly.

Other policy opportunities include:

- Removing higher mileage rates for larger cars.

- Incentivising the purchase of low carbon vehicles for company cars.

- Implementing a mileage rate for cycling.

- Adding extra checks and balances to the purchase of hazardous materials, while providing lists of non-hazardous alternatives.

Identifying problems and opportunities

The best way to identify opportunities to shape the working environment to foster good behaviour is to ask your employees. Why do they follow certain paths? What would help them change? Front-line staff in particular often have a completely different view of how a company operates (some would say they know how it really operates).

This process can be combined with 'making people part of the solution' covered in Chapter 4. In fact, when I do staff engagement sessions with clients, I always offer the option of capturing ideas generated and feeding them back into the clients' business improvement processes. This has the added benefit of demonstrating that the solutions generation sessions are meaningful as participants can see their ideas being taken seriously.

Questions for you

Which green technologies would give your employees the opportunity to pursue greener behaviour?

How can you alter the physical layout of your working environment to promote green behaviour?

How can you alter bureaucratic processes and policies to promote green behaviour?

What perverse incentives will need to be flipped around?

How can you get the right insight into working life to identify these opportunities?

CHAPTER 6

Human Resources Issues

WHILE THE GREEN JUJITSU APPROACH is very powerful for culture change, it will work best within a human resources (HR) structure designed to promote sustainability. In this chapter we will consider some of the supporting functions which can be altered to maximise its effectiveness. As we will see, there are also opportunities to embed the Green Jujitsu approach into that HR structure.

Recruitment

It is a truism that organisations are groups of people rather than entities in their own right. If you want a particular culture, then recruiting people whose attitudes are compatible with sustainability makes a good foundation for your efforts. However, I have found that it is generally easier to teach a good engineer about sustainability than it is to teach an environmental expert about engineering.

The good news is that companies with a good reputation on environmental and ethical issues have been shown to attract more applicants, so you will have more to choose from, which makes it more likely that you will find candidates who are great at their job and interested in sustainability.

To maximise this opportunity, sustainability issues should be incorporated into the whole recruitment process. Examples include:

- Pre-application information, for example, the 'Working at ACME plc' section of the website.

- Application briefing and job description (see below).

- Questions on application forms and interview process.

- Content of orientation tours, etc.

This will warm up new recruits so they arrive with an idea of the company culture they will be working in.

Job descriptions and performance assessment

One of the biggest mistakes an organisation can make is to have a misalignment between responsibility and authority when it comes to sustainability. If you want to give someone responsibility for a particular aspect of sustainability, then they must have the authority to act. Traditionally, environmental managers have had huge amounts of responsibility (including keeping their bosses out of jail) but precious little authority.

Clearly, the most effective way to fix this disconnect is to give specific sustainability responsibilities to those who already have sufficient authority to act – people such as site managers, production managers and heads of procurement. This integration of sustainability into core jobs is a leap away from the traditional environmental manager beavering away fruitlessly in his or her green silo.

It follows that if you give someone responsibility and authority, you must also give them accountability. So the responsibility must be backed up with targets which should be reviewed in performance assessment. This is particularly important for middle management who tend to be very target oriented.

Formal training

Training sessions are a great opportunity to promote environmental sustainability to individuals. Green Jujitsu techniques can be incorporated into training itself:

- Incorporating sustainability into as many 'mainstream' training courses as possible, particularly induction training, so it is seen to be part of the mainstream and not a fringe topic.

- Tailor sustainability training to job roles to make it as relevant as possible to individuals' daily routine.

- Use storytelling in case studies to show how sustainability is driven by 'people like us'.

- Use exercises to get participants to generate sustainability solutions to drive relevance and buy-in to the process.

Who does the changing?

One of the biggest questions is whether to form a sustainability team or not, and how that team should be constituted. There are four main options, all but the last can be mixed and matched:

- Formal, dedicated sustainability staff team.

- Part-time staff committee: volunteer members who have 'day jobs' but meet periodically to review and monitor progress.

- Part-time sustainability, green or energy 'champions' who are asked to encourage sustainability in their immediate working environment.

- No team: either use a facilitator to work with staff across business functions or the 'benign dictatorship' approach of small companies with strong and determined leaders.

The advantages of the four systems are given in Table 2.

TABLE 2: Advantages of different staffing approaches.

Dedicated team	Part-time committee	Sustainability champions	No team
Ensures required expertise in house	Cross-section of functions represented	Cross-section of functions represented	Ownership with mainstream employees
Defined responsibility and accountability	Buy-in ensured	Cheaper than formal team – only part-time requirement of staff time	No 'us and them' ghettoisation of 'green'
More projects can be launched and monitored	Centre of gravity around which activity can take place	Local 'experts' can apply their domain knowledge	Agile – no bureaucracy
Less chance of issues 'falling between stools'	Much cheaper than formal team in terms of salaries	Peer-to-peer communications may be better trusted	Cheap – no bureaucracy
	Can be effective in a 'leadership vacuum'		

Different companies use different combinations of these approaches depending on their company culture. Whichever approach is adopted, it is important that the individuals are trained in the Green Jujitsu approach. One approach that is widely misused, in my opinion, is the use of 'champions', so we will look at that in more detail.

Sustainability/environmental champions

One of the most common first steps large organisations make in sustainability programmes is to appoint sustainability champions throughout the functions and ranks. The usual argument for doing so is that champions are embedded into the organisation and can provide peer-to-peer support to other staff members who want change their behaviour and act as local flag-wavers for corporate green goals.

This is great in theory, but peer-to-peer by definition is bottom-up, appointing people to roles is top-down and I believe that is a fundamental conflict. I've also seen the champion role seriously abused. I've seen junior volunteers given energy efficiency targets for entire sites, I've seen them (post-volunteering) being expected to read energy meters on a regular basis, and I've heard of them being expected to get into work before everyone else to check who has switched their computers off. As a result of this lack of definition, many champion programmes descend into forums for complaint.

So what's the alternative? Well, if you want to engage with green thinking people, why not create a club to glean their ideas and share what is happening in the organisation? Then the peer-to-peer communication will come out organically rather than the artificial champion version.

The other option is to appoint green champions, but give them a well-defined role and training in Green Jujitsu-style behavioural change. Involve them in company-wide engagement programmes as facilitators and solutions generators, but don't expect them to work miracles on your behalf.

External change agents

There are advantages in employing an external change agent such as a consultant to engage with employees:

- A lack of baggage: external people do not bring with them the toxic effects of office politics, prejudices or bad blood that internal change agents may be saddled with.

- External agents generally come with a breadth of experience from working with a wide range of organisations which can help provoke or stimulate new thinking.

- Culture change is difficult and specialist skills are required to get the programme off on the right foot.

The disadvantages of using an external agent are:

- It can be difficult to walk onto someone else's patch and persuade them to change what they are doing without getting a negative reaction. However, there are tools and techniques to overcome this (see Annex A).

- It can be difficult to hand over to permanent staff without loss of momentum, but long-term ownership must reside within the organisation.

Questions for you

Does your recruitment process get the right message over to potential recruits?

Is responsibility aligned to authority and vice versa in your organisation?

Do you incorporate sustainability into 'mainstream' training, for example, induction courses?

Does your formal sustainability training utilise Green Jujitsu techniques?

Do your change agents have the necessary Green Jujitsu skills and experiences?

Could an external change agent help?

Conclusions

CULTURE CHANGE IS WIDELY REGARDED as the single biggest challenge for organisations wishing to embrace sustainability. The standard response to this challenge is often primitive – switch it off stickers, awareness posters and clichéd proclamations from the great and the good – and ultimately ineffective.

The Green Jujitsu approach presented in this e-book is incredibly powerful, but subtle. It is all about understanding your audience, gauging their strengths and interests, and tailoring your programme to exploit those strengths and interests. While this may appear on the face of it to be obvious, it is worth noting that most sustainability culture change programmes take the exact opposite approach.

We have covered a whole toolbox of Green Jujitsu techniques within the elephant/rider/path model of culture change:

- The rider: tailoring the message to the rider, rather than expecting the rider to become 'converted'.

- The elephant: engaging on a deeper emotional level by truly involving individuals in the process.

- The path: altering the working environment and rules to encourage green behaviour and discourage ungreen behaviour.

My favoured technique across all three aspects of the elephant model is to involve all employees in solutions generation. This can identify problems and opportunities in informing the rider and shaping the path, all the while inspiring the elephant.

So, once you start implementing the Green Jujitsu approach, how do you know if your efforts are working? You should look out for the following telltale signs:

- People look pleased to see you.

- Colleagues start knocking on your door to ask your advice.

- Colleagues start knocking on your door with new suggestions.

- Your key performance indicators start improving faster than you expected.

- The boss takes a genuine interest.

- Spontaneous projects start springing up all over your organisation and you struggle to keep up with them.

- Other people start trying to muscle in and/or take credit.

- Your staff start bragging about the company's achievements.

- New recruits tell you that the organisation's green efforts attracted them to the business.

To start seeing these signs of progress takes a lot of work – working harder and smarter. The Green Jujitsu approach requires a certain amount of humility, a huge amount of astuteness and, above all, an infinite supply of perseverance. Whatever you do, however hard it can seem at times, keep going, keep trying stuff, keep thinking and keep doing what works.

ANNEX

Group Exercises

Overview

THIS ANNEX GIVES SOME INSIGHT into how I run group engagement sessions. Clearly, different people will want to adapt this to maximise their own strengths and circumstances, but this is the way I maximise the benefits of the Green Jujitsu approach.

Powerpoint or not?

A wag once said 'all power corrupts, but PowerPoint corrupts absolutely'. While I often use this useful technology to illustrate my talks and to back up my longer training sessions, I am increasingly trying to eradicate PowerPoint from my shorter stakeholder engagement sessions whether for employees or external people. I have run many sessions with up to 40 delegates with just a flipchart, a marker pen, a selection of Post-Its and some A0 prints of my brainstorming tools.

The problems with using PowerPoint are:

- Audiences are now indoctrinated with the idea that once the screen goes up they can sit back in their chair and go into passive listening mode or go into critic mode.

- It can be difficult to switch between 'presentation mode' and 'interactive mode'.

- PowerPoint can be horribly misused with reams of bullet point laden slides.

Setting PowerPoint aside can make for a refreshing change.

Gaining immediate buy-in

My standard opening for an engagement session is to stand beside a blank flipchart sheet and ask 'Why are we here?' I quickly explain that I don't mean in a metaphysical sense, but why is the organisation interested in sustainability (or whatever subset of sustainability we are working with).

There are a number of reasons for starting like this:

- You throw the delegates straight into the issue, before they have time to sit back and cross their arms.

- They sell the business case for sustainability (and the need for the session) to themselves and each other, rather than you having to try to persuade them.

- You get a flavour of the thinking of the delegates so you can tweak the tone and content of the rest of the session to match.

I write their responses up on a flip chart and keep asking them for more until they've got all the most important ones. The knack is not to be afraid of silence – ask 'anything else' and wait, marker poised until someone speaks up. Once we have finished, I leave the flipchart up as it is often useful to refer back to it later on in the session.

Solutions generation

The process revolves around the Terra Infirma Brainstorming tool (see Figure 3). This has been designed to give some structure to brainstorming without throttling the conversation. It basically gives four generic ways of contributing to an environmental goal at the head of the fishbone diagram. The top two are about doing the right thing, the bottom two about doing things right. The left-hand two are about people and the right-hand two are about hardware. So the four are:

- Procedures (people doing the right thing): are the official procedures designed to allow and encourage the desired behaviour of staff members (or others)? Do they discourage or bar undesired behaviour? How would they need to change?

- Behaviour (people doing things right): are people actually behaving in the right way? What training might they need? What techniques from Chapters 4 and 5 would encourage them to behave differently?

- Technology (the right hardware): do you have the right equipment, software and/or materials? What would make a positive difference?

- Application (hardware being applied correctly): has that technology been installed and set up correctly? Is it being maintained properly? (The actual operation of the equipment would come under Procedures and Behaviour.)

Just to take the example of a compressed air system:

- If the compressor itself needs upgrading, that solution would come under Technology.

- If the airlines are not being checked for leaks, the solutions would come under Application.

- If the compressed air is being misused such as squirting fellow employees, then a formal rule banning this would come under Procedures.

- Behaviour solutions could include providing feedback on the amount of compressed air being used and how much it costs.

Here's how I will typically use the tool:

- Customise a version of the tool for each of your organisations' sustainability targets by writing the target in the 'head' of the fishbone (e.g. Carbon Neutral, Zero Waste).

- Print one copy of each version on an A0 sheet and stick the sheets around the walls of the training room.

- Split the delegates into teams of at least three per team, introduce the tool and assign a team to each sheet.

- Give each team a different colour of Post-It notes and challenge them to think of solutions, write each one on a Post-It and stick it to the appropriate part of the brainstorming tool.

- After 8–15 minutes, rotate the teams so each has a different sheet. Using the same colour of Post-It as they had before, challenge them to think of solutions that the previous team(s) hadn't thought of.

- Continue rotating the teams until every team has had a go at each sheet which should now be covered in a rainbow of Post-Its.

- Challenge the teams to pick the best three solutions they have thought of across the different sheets.

The A0 sheets are highly effective. They are fresh and novel for most participants, a big group can crowd around them, they encourage a more kinaesthetic approach to the problem, and the big sheet takes a lot of filling with Post-Its, encouraging more ideas. The rotation means that the exercise gets more and more difficult as time goes on, making teams think harder and keeping their attention.

FIGURE 3. Terra Infirma Brainstorming tool.

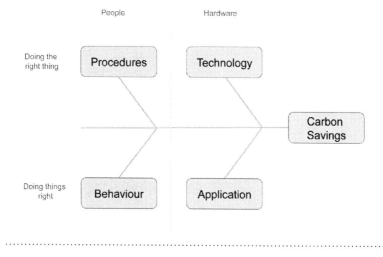

References

1. Amory Lovins, Rocky Mountain Institute, speaking at Schumacher College, Devon, 2002.

2. Kane, G. 2011. *The Green Executive: Corporate Leadership for a Low Carbon Economy* (London: Earthscan).

3. Figure adapted from Thompson, M., Ellis, R. and Widavsky, A. 1990. *Cultural Theory* (Boulder, CO: Westview Press).

4. Heath, C. and Heath, D. 2010. *Switch: How to Change Things When Change is Hard* (New York: Random House Business).

5. For more on this, see Senge, P.M., Smith, B., Schley, S., Laur, J. and Kruschwitz, N. 2008. *The Necessary Revolution: How Individuals and Organizations are Working Together to Create a Sustainable World* (London: Nicholas Brearley Publishing).

6. See http://www.energysavingtrust.org.uk/In-your-home/Your-energy-supply/Smart-meters.

7. Anderson, R. 2010. *Confessions of a Radical Industrialist: How Interface Proved That You Can Build a Successful Business without Destroying the Planet* (London: Random House Business).

8. Bennis, W. 1999. The leadership advantage. *Leader To Leader* (No. 12, Spring), http://www.leadertoleader.org/knowledgecenter/journal.aspx?ArticleID=53.

9. See   http://www.dailymail.co.uk/sciencetech/article-1301713/The-crack-roof-world-Yes-global-warming-real--deeply-worrying.html.

10. Ashley Lodge, Harper Collins, speaking at the Low Carbon Innovation Exchange, London, 26 June 2008.

REFERENCES

11. See http://www.deliverfreedom.com/blog/offices-going-green-funny-email-taglines/.

12. Thaler, R.H. and Sunstein, C.R. 2008. *Nudge: Improving Decisions about Health, Wealth and Happiness* (London: Penguin).

Lightning Source UK Ltd.
Milton Keynes UK
UKOW05f1302231213

223557UK00002B/43/P